STORIES FROM

HELL

A Mom's Memorable Moments

HELEN MCLAUGHLIN

American Literary Press, Inc.
Five Star Special Edition
Baltimore, Maryland

Stories from Hell: A Mom's Memorable Moments

Library of Congress
Cataloging in Publication Data
ISBN 1-56167-402-8

Library of Congress Card Catalog Number:
98-85213

Published by

American Literary Press, Inc.
Five Star Special Edition
8019 Belair Road, Suite 10
Baltimore, Maryland 21236

Manufactured in the United States of America

To Harry, Jeffrey, Kevin, Timothy,
Dennis and Keith without whom my
life would have been very dull.

To my daughters-in-law and best friends
Jane and Tracy for their encouragement
and the title.

To Cory, Max, Esther, Harry, Shannon,
Gray and Charlie. Something to remember
me by.

A special thanks to Roy Pierce
for his time, patience and expertise
in preparing this book for print.

Table of Contents

1. HELL'S STORY

Things happen to my family on a consistent basis that don't happen to other families in their entire lifetime. As I am writing this book, my son, Kevin (now 38), is laying on our recliner chair with casts on both legs and his right hand. He was hit by a car while walking home four days before Christmas. He has no hospitalization and the man who hit him has no automobile insurance. He lives in Maryland, is single, and has no one else to take care of him.

Everyone wants to be remembered for something during their lifetime. I want to be remembered for this profound advice that I am about to offer you. MAKE SURE ALL OF YOUR CHILDREN ARE MARRIED, OR REMARRIED, BEFORE YOU TURN 60!

It appears that I will be homebound for the next several months. What better time to recall the other major incidents in my life that caused utter havoc?

It all started in 1956 when our first son, Jeff, was born in Georgetown Hospital. My sister lent us her Cadillac to drive him home from the hospital. Nothing but the best for our firstborn. It even had air conditioning. How's that for class?

Our second son, Kevin, was due on December 31, 1957. My husband, who I shall refer to as Our Father, totaled our car on his way home from work on Christmas Eve. A friend lent us his beat up old Ford since birthing was imminent. The heater didn't even work. When it became apparent that our little tax deduction wasn't going to arrive on time, Our Father would drive off the side of the road to stir things up. It didn't work. He wasn't born until January 5th and he came home from the hospital in a "has been" with no heat.

Tim, Dennis and Keith arrived in yearly increments at Georgetown. The same doctor, nurses and aides tended to me with that "not you again" look in their eyes. When Keith was born we named our house "Boystown."

1

People always told me when my children were small they were little problems but when they grow up they are big problems. No truer words were ever spoken. My sister-in-law often told friends that I would probably have a nervous breakdown but I just didn't have the time. That's true, too.

When Keith entered first grade my life changed. I couldn't stand the peace and quiet. After they left for school I would clean the house spotless. It would stay that way all day until the earthquake struck at 4:00. They would knock each other over trying to get through the door. Books were thrown on the dining room table, the refrigerator flew open, glasses came out of cabinets and crumbs went on the floor. Then they were off to their rooms where uniforms went on the floor, clothes fell out of drawers, the TV was on, the stereo blaring and the phone was ringing off the hook. I couldn't handle it. I went to work.

I chose employment in the school system so I was off on school holidays and all summer. Every Monday during those seventeen years the lunch bunch would ask, "Well, what did they do this weekend?", and I would entertain them with my Stories from Hell!

2. OLD HAT

Shortly after Keith was born my namesake, Aunt Helen, called and announced she was coming to visit our newborn. Aunt Helen was very prim and proper. This meant the house had to be in perfect condition, not to mention myself and the four children. I always referred to her visits as, "The Inspector General is coming." My sister, Kay, volunteered to drive her.

I had a doctor's appointment that afternoon for my six week checkup. My mother was accompanying me so she could supervise the four boys in the doctor's waiting room.

Kay arrived with two of her seven children, aged 4 and nine months, and Aunt Helen. The Inspector General only had one child so she was beside herself with six children running around. When the ordeal was over and the Inspector General was ready to leave, her hat was missing. She just couldn't understand why the children would hide her hat. We looked everywhere. We interrogated all of the children. No one admitted to hiding her hat. My doctor's appointment was getting closer and I was getting more nervous by the minute. After searching for thirty minutes we finally found it where it had fallen -- behind the sofa. It was now time to pack Mother and the four children into the car and depart for the doctor appointment. We all left together and said our good-byes walking to the cars.

Kay and the Inspector General were driving behind me. When we got about ten blocks away Kay started blowing her horn. I looked in the rear view mirror and they appeared to be waving to us so my mother and I waved to them and continued on. At the next intersection Kay pulled right up beside us. She was frantic. Her nine month old was still in my house! We did an about face and returned to my home.

When you put snowsuits on babies, you lay them on the

floor, put the baby in and zip them up. We opened the front door and there was Jimmy with his arms and legs stretched out just as she left him on the living room floor. Of course, we all had to come into the house because the Inspector General had wet her pants over the whole scenario.

That wasn't the only time my sister left her baby. When Jimmy was three she took him to the supermarket. She loaded the groceries in the car and drove home. While she was carrying the groceries into the kitchen the store manager called. She inquired, "Did I leave some of my packages there?" He said, "No, you left your child here!"

I only had five children and I know what it's like to pack clothing, toys, diapers, port-a-cribs, beach supplies, etc. and load up the car to go on vacation. You look like Gypsies driving down the road. We have close friends who have nine children. They took them all to Ocean City on vacation. She kept telling her husband, "I feel like we forgot something." You know the male response to that one. "Look at this car. How could we possibly have forgotten something?" As they were crossing the Bay Bridge, she turned to him and said, "Frank, we left the baby home in the crib!"

3. MUMPS MANEUVER

At the end of the school term when Jeff was in kindergarten, he contacted mumps. Our Father was quite concerned because if you get mumps when you're older it can cause monumental complications. In addition to that if the other four siblings were to catch them one at a time it could stretch out through the summer and our annual vacation would be down the drain. We were always very germ conscious. So much so that each of the boys had their own different colored mug to drink out of. Everyone knew their color plus each of their brother's 5 colors and no one dared to drink out of anyone else's cup.

Our Father had a brainstorm. It would be more sensible for the boys to catch mumps while they were young and all at the same time so as not to ruin our vacation. He summoned the four siblings to Jeff's bedside where he poured Coca Cola into Jeff's cup and invited each to drink out of it. Well, that immediately caused a stir as they were adamant that they were not drinking out of the forbidden Jeff's cup. We were very satisfied with our clandestine operation until the following morning when Jeff broke out with chickenpox.

Fourteen days later I embarked on the Childhood Disease Disaster of my life. Can you imagine a 4 year old, 2 1/2 year old, 1 1/2 year old and an 8 month old with chickenpox and mumps together simultaneously? And they were sick, sick, sick! I had to keep a chart of their temperatures, what time each one had baby aspirin, who needed to be doused with Calamine lotion, etc. I lived through the ordeal but would never recommend the coke in the cup method to anyone in their right mind.

Tim developed some blisters on the right side of his chest when he was six. It was a small cluster at first but was spreading rapidly across one of his ribs. I thought it was impetigo but made an appointment with the pediatrician. He was amazed to discover that Tim had shingles. He had never seen a case on a child so young so he called in all the other pediatricians in the medical building to look at him. He was on display for quite a while.

The doctor explained that shingles is a chickenpox virus that usually attacks adults whose immunity had worn off. His explanation for Tim having acquired shingles was the fact that he had chickenpox and mumps at the same time. He apparently had a mild case of chickenpox and his immunity had already expired. He was in bed for ten days. The blisters followed a nerve and went all the way around to the center of his back.

Tim was playing basketball on our patio in his teens with his shirt off. Our next-door neighbor, Becky, asked him how he got the scar. He replied, "From shingles." She said, "Oh, did they fall off the roof?"

4. PLAYING FOOTSIES

Our first home was on a corner lot in the suburbs with traffic in front of the house and also on the side street. Our Father insisted we needed to move to the country where it would be safer to raise five sons. He also said we couldn't have a dog until we moved to the country because it would be run over by a car. When we became serious about moving we decided to sell the house ourselves (no outrageous real estate commissions for us!). After a year of no takers we turned the house over to a real estate company. In the meantime, we fell in love with several houses in the country. We would make an offer contingent upon selling our home. Every few months we would lose a house because we hadn't sold ours. After a year of real estate expertise, we finally had a buyer.

The contract on our house was subject to FHA approval. I was worried to death that the FHA wouldn't appraise the house for the price we were asking. The day finally arrived for the FHA appraiser to inspect our house. I met him at the door with the five little ones wrapped around my legs and body. Dennis immediately asked the man, "Did you get my letter?" He responded, "No, I didn't get your letter." Dennis said, "Oh, I guess I forgot to stamp it." and with that he took his little foot and stamped on the man's foot as hard as he could. What happened next was more than I could begin to imagine. The man started moaning and groaning and had to sit down on the stairs and hold his foot and rub it. Then he said, "Thank God it wasn't my other foot because I have ingrown toenails." My heart sank. I knew we were never going to be able to sell our house.

He finally managed to get up and complete the inspection. The six of us followed him around, room by room, like a gaggle of geese, until the inspection was completed. I just kept praying that he wouldn't let the foot incident influence his final appraisal. As he prepared to leave and before I could do a thing to stop it, I heard the horror words repeated and this time he got the ingrown toenails.

I didn't know how I was going to explain this to Our Father when he got home from work. Our moving prospects were now crushed like the appraiser's toes.

5.   BLACK CATS ON HALLOWEEN

We took the boys to the Church Bazaar and Our Father gave them each fifty cents to spend as they pleased. (Fifty cents was a lot of money in 1965.) Four of the boys spent their money wisely but Kevin happened by a booth that was selling kittens for fifty cents each. That was our first family pet named Clancy. By the time summer arrived Clancy had six kittens. We tried exceptionally hard to dispose of these six kittens.

When Halloween rolled around, they were still living with Clancy. Then someone hit on this great idea. We would give them away to the Trick or Treaters on Halloween. If you could have seen the little costumed faces light up when they were handed a darling black kitten. You would have thought we had given them a million dollars.

Unfortunately, by the time the last kitten was disposed of, the first parent's car pulled up to our door. As the breaks screeched to a halt we knew we were in deep shit! We were in for quite a tongue lashing. It didn't take long for the other five parents to follow suit.

We thought it was a good idea but the following year we bought candy for the Trick or Treaters. For some strange reason, no one came to our door!

6. SURROGATE GRANDPARENTS

When we first moved to Howard County our closest and only neighbors were at the end of our dead end road. The McKnights, who were older, eventually became our best friends. Vi and Mac had moved there several years before our house was built. Their children were grown and they became surrogate grandparents to our five.

I have so many fond memories of our dear friends. They had a horse, Misty, and a pony, Twinkles. During our first year there Mac would occasionally pay the boys a dollar for cleaning out his horse stalls. They would happily shovel the manure for hours on a Saturday for their pay. The first time we had watermelon the next summer I told the boys that you always make a wish the first time you eat watermelon each year. I almost fell over when Keith, who was 4, confided in me that he wished that Mr. McKnight would ask them to clean out his stalls soon.

Christmas that year was probably the most exciting of their lives. We had invited the McKnights to share Christmas dinner with us on Christmas Eve. It couldn't have been a more perfect Christmas since it was snowing and breathtaking to look out over acres and acres of white velvet.

The McKnights arrived with a humongous box all wrapped with a huge bow on top. The card said, To: Jeff, Kevin, Tim, Dennis and Keith. They could hardly eat dinner for eyeing that box and wondering what it contained. To be honest I was equally as curious. When it was time to exchange gifts they tore off the wrapping in unison and were flabbergasted to find a beautiful leather saddle inside. The payoff came when Mac announced that because of the snow he wasn't able to bring the rest of the gift to them. It was their pony, Twinkling Twilight (alias Twinkles). They were in a state of shock. Kevin fell on the floor flat on his back.

Of course, this wonderful childhood gift spelled only one

thing to Our Father -- W-O-R-K! He had to build a barn or shelter of some type and fence in a corral. He had already built a playhouse on top of four telephone poles so he enclosed underneath and presto Twinkles had a home. He spent every evening and weekends hand digging post holes for the fence.
When he only had a few more holes to dig to fence in the acre, an older 4-H member rode by on his horse. I'll never forget the expression on Our Father's face when he announced his father had an attachment to his tractor and he would have gladly done those holes for ten cents apiece.

Each Christmas after Twinkles, the McKnights outdid themselves with one appropriate gift for all five. The following year it was a toboggan, and then a unicycle, a regulation leather punching bag and two pair of boxing gloves, and on and on.

When they became teenagers it became more and more difficult to come up with ideas. One year they received a huge box (almost as big as the saddle box) filled with Vi's homemade Christmas cookies. They dropped the gift off before leaving to spend Christmas in Oklahoma with their daughter. They gave specific instructions that it couldn't be opened until Christmas Eve. They honored the request but by Christmas night every cookie had been devoured. I thought it was quite a compliment that the cookies disappeared so quickly so the morning after I sent a telegram to Oklahoma, "PLEASE SEND MORE COOKIES." The next day we received a telegram. It said, "SORRY, OUT OF DOUGH!"

The McKnights always had a Christmas Tree Party several weeks before Christmas. Everyone would meet at their house and then drive separately in a caravan to a Christmas tree farm about 15 miles away. It was great fun for the whole family tramping through the woods in search of the perfect tree. Everyone had their own idea as to what constituted a perfect tree. The weather usually determined that. If it was an un-usually warm December day, it could take up to an hour and a half to find it. But if it was nasty cold and windy that perfect tree could be determined in less than five minutes. Everyone would put their tree on top of their car and drive back to the

McKnights. Our car occupants would join in singing carols all the way back. Vi would always have hot buttered rum for the adults and Cokes for the kids, not to mention a buffet fit for a king.

One year Mac put up his outdoor Christmas lights the first Sunday in December since it was a nice warm day. That naturally ignited our boys to start bugging us to put our lights up. I explained that it was just the first Sunday in Advent and it is a time of penance to prepare us for the celebration of the beautiful feast of the birth of Christ. The next day, after departing the school bus in front of the McKnight's house, Keith knocked on their door. When Vi greeted him, he said, "Mrs. McKnight, I hate to tell you this but it's only the first week of Advent and you shouldn't have your Christmas lights on." She thanked him profusely and ran to the phone and called me. They never lit them again until ours were lit.

Vi always marveled at the fact that when the five little McLaughlin boys got on the school bus in the morning they looked like Beau Brummell. They were neat and clean with every hair in place. But when they stepped off that bus in the afternoon their shirttails were out, no neckties, hair messed up, you name it.

Another thing that amazed her was that our dog, Kelly, would wait with them for the bus to arrive. As the bus stopped, she would walk out into the road and stand guard until the door closed and then she would get out of the road and walk back up the street to our house. The most amazing thing was that about thirty minutes before the bus brought them home, she would walk down the street and lay on the corner until they returned home. Again she would stand guard until all five were off the bus. Apparently, her sensitive ears could hear the bus five miles away. That's the only logical explanation for her knowing when to go meet the bus.

I was always a worry wort but one of my most horrible fears was that there would be a school bus accident and my whole family could be wiped out. That never entered my mind when the whole family was riding in the station wagon, only when they were on the school bus.

One day Dennis stopped to visit Vi while she was working in her garden. He told her that her flowers were pretty but his mother grows "Bastard Buttons" in her garden!

The McKnights had a cabin in the Virginia mountains they referred to as The Shack. They invited the family to join them at their retreat. On the way to The Shack we stopped at a gas station in Winchester. I sat in the car while Our Father and all of the boys used the Men's Room. The first one back in the car said, "Ugh, yuck, the toilet was filled with bread." The second one got in the car and said, "Ugh, yuck, you couldn't flush the toilet because it was filled with bread." The third and fourth got in the car and repeated it again. I said to myself, "If one more kid gets in this car and mentions the bread I'm going to scream." The fifth one got in but before I blew my top Our Father exited the Men's Room. While we were all watching, he stood in front of the Men's Room door and pretended to be chewing (the bread, of course). We all nearly fell out of the car laughing.

The Shack was nice but there was no electricity. It did, however, have an indoor chemical toilet. There was a small lake nearby for swimming. It was the boys first experience at "roughing it" with no lights, TV, radio, etc. We cooked our meals outdoors over a campfire and boiled water for bathing.

The first day at The Shack wasn't what I had hoped for. Our Father and Jeff had words and Jeff ran away. I had visions of him lost in the woods and being attacked by bears and other wild animals. Our Father and the McKnights sort of took it in stride. They figured he would come home when it got dark. I didn't share their lack of concern. After all, it was my baby out there lost in the woods alone, starving. The brothers, on the other hand, could care less. If he didn't come back it was just one less mouth to feed and more for them to eat. As the sun started to set, my heart started to sink. Just as I was getting all prayed out, I spotted him slowly coming down the mountain.

The rest of the vacation was much more enjoyable. We would hike down the mountain and swim and hike back up and eat. We spent the evenings playing cards with a kerosene lamp in the middle of the table. One year we took a portable radio and listened in the darkness to Neil Armstrong's famous "One small step for man. One giant step for mankind." I'm sure none of us will ever forget that.

Twinkles and the boys.

7. DOGGONE SHAME

We were living in the country surrounded by acres of open land. It was time for the long awaited dog. I piled the boys into the station wagon and headed for the animal shelter. I didn't have the faintest idea how complicated animal adoption could be. I actually thought I was doing them a favor by taking a dog off their hands.

I had to fill out a form and sign an affidavit that stipulated:

a. No child under three years of age lived at the residence.

b. The residence had a fenced in yard. We had to get a special exception permit for this. Once they verified we had two acres of land we would qualify.

c. The animal had to be spayed before six months of age.

We went from cage to cage and finally selected a mixed Shepherd female puppy. She was tan and fluffy with some black markings. We named her Kelly. No one wanted to get near her in the car because she smelled so bad.

We only had Kelly for three weeks when Our Father came into the house and announced, "Helen, you're dog is dead! I knew it was going to happen. I told you to keep her from running behind the car."

That day had been horrendous from the very beginning. It was a Sunday. We all came out and got in the car to go to Church and then realized we had a flat tire. We got out of the station wagon and squeezed into the Corvair. When we backed out of the carport we ran over Tim's bike which was inappropriately standing behind the car. Some days you wonder if you really should go to Church.

After Church the boys went down to the Patuxent River about a mile down the road. It wasn't long before Tim came running home. He had cut the top of his head under the rusty bridge. Our Father put a butterfly on it and he went off to join his brothers. Our Father put the flat tire in the trunk of the Corvair and ran over Kelly.

16

I was in tears when I ran to the carport. Kelly was laying under the tire. I yelled, "The least you could do is back the car off of her." He moved the car and I thought I saw her move. Our Father said, "Rigor mortis is setting in. I better bury her before the boys come home and see her." When he went to get the shovel, Kelly dragged herself across the carport. She lived for seven years with tire tracks on her ribs.

8. MONKEY BUSINESS

Our Ophthalmologist was about 25 miles away in a medical park in Bowie. Kevin had new glasses and the doctor needed to check them and I needed an eye examination. I had no choice but to take the whole family. He checked out Kevin's new glasses and it was my turn to go in for the examination. The boys asked if they could go to the shopping center across the street while I was being treated. I was apprehensive but out of consideration for the other folks in the waiting room I thought it might be best if they left.

Their first stop was the Pet Shop. It didn't take long for the five of them to spot a monkey in the back of the store. There was a big sign: DO NOT GET NEAR THE MONKEY IF YOU WEAR EYEGLASSES. Immediately the monkey reached through the cage, grabbed Kevin's glasses and proceeded to jump up and down on them before depositing them under the newspaper in his cage. The brothers were in hysterics because they knew Kevin was in deep trouble. They didn't want to tell the manager because of his warning sign but there was no way the monkey was parting with his cache. After a lecture from the manager he was able to retrieve them.

When I came out of the doctor's office they were waiting. There was Kevin with his glasses zigzagging across his face and four brothers smiling from ear to ear. The urge to kill was strong within but I managed to keep my cool and Speak No Evil. It could have been worse. They could have bought the monkey.

9. ASSESSOR PRESSURE

When the county announced they would be reassessing property, Our Father gave me specific instructions as to what I was to do when the assessor knocked on our door. First of all I was not to allow him to come into the house. I was to stand at the front door and answer all of his questions. Above all, I was to make sure he did not walk around to the back of the house. I was confident I could handle the assessor brilliantly.

The downstairs was completely out of ground on the back of the house. Our Father was in the process of finishing a paneled bedroom with seating area, built-in desks and bath for Jeff, Kevin and Tim. If the assessor were to walk around the house and look into a window he might see this along with the basketball court and barn. Our Father was adamant that since the renovation wasn't complete and we weren't using the bedroom and bath that we shouldn't have to pay taxes for it. As far as the basketball court and barn were concerned, "What he didn't know wouldn't hurt him!"

By the time the assessor arrived school was out and all the boys were home to meet him at the door. Our dog, Kelly, didn't care for strangers or assessors. Kelly followed him to our door barking viciously. The assessor seemed very uneasy so I figured it would be a quick visit and he certainly wouldn't dare walk around the house. He asked how many bedrooms, bathrooms and fireplaces we had. I assured him we had three bedrooms, two baths and one fireplace. He inquired if the downstairs was unfinished and I emphatically replied, "Yes." Dennis immediately burst out with, "Mommy, you forgot about the big new bedroom Daddy is building downstairs." The assessor looked at me and I sheepishly said, "Oh, does that count? It's not finished." He wrote something down on his clipboard and commented, "I was going to walk around the house but I don't think your dog will allow it." With that, Tim flew out the door, grabbed Kelly's collar and said, "I'll hold her

19

for you." I'm sure I don't have to tell you we got slapped with the Mother of all Tax Assessments that year.

10. SCHOOL DAZE

Sister Agneta taught the fifth grade at St. Louis School. She had to put up with all five McLaughlins. She knew us well! When Kevin was in the fifth grade he was going to Notre Dame. He started his "educator fund" with his nickels and dimes. One of Sr. Agneta's ex-students was on Notre Dame's basketball team. When she heard that Notre Dame was going to be playing a game in Baltimore she struck up a deal with the class. The boy that tried the hardest, behaved the best, etc. would be selected to accompany her to the Notre Dame game.

Kevin was determined he was going to that game. I tried to prepare him for the disappointment if he didn't get picked but he wouldn't hear of it. When the big day arrived, Kevin went to the Notre Dame game. Afterwards, they went to the locker room and got autographs from all of the players.

Everything between Sr. Agneta and the McLaughlin group wasn't peaches and cream. I'll never forget the time she sent Dennis home with a note for me to sign. The note explained that Dennis had given a classmate a "wedgey." She was disgusted and wanted to be sure that we took the proper action to see that it never happened again. I really couldn't get too worked up over a wedgey but I did caution Dennis never to do it again. When he went to bed he laid the note on the kitchen table for me to sign, which I did. Unbeknownst to me, Our Father also signed the note.

I received a call at work the following day from Sr. Agneta. She was so mad she was seeing stars. She kept saying, "I don't think it's a bit funny." I had no idea what she was talking about. She was talking about what Our Father had written on the note. He wrote, "I gave Helen a wedgey and she liked it!"

Students at St. Louis wore uniforms which included a plaid necktie. Dennis forgot his tie one day. He didn't want to get into trouble so he made one. He cut a tie out of loose leaf paper and pinned it on the front of his shirt. Sr. Agneta's note to me said, "Dennis wore this tie to school today. I think you can afford a better one." The tie was enclosed.

When Keith got to the fifth grade, sex education was introduced into the curriculum. The school set aside a Friday night in January for fathers and sons to attend a sex education meeting. It was the same night as the CYO Track Meet at the University of Maryland. I had already purchased the tickets. Naturally, we all went to the track meet. Monday, Keith came home with a note from Sister. She wanted to know why Our Father and Keith did not attend the sex education meeting. Our Father wrote back, "We took our sons to the CYO Track Meet. We feel sports are more important than sex."

11. LUNCH, ANYONE?

One morning I emerged from the shower and noticed I was covered with a rash. Since I worked in a school with four hundred children I realized I might have something contagious and certainly wouldn't want to expose innocent children to what I had. All I could think of was my rash as I prepared the boys' lunches, called them for breakfast and hurried them along so they wouldn't miss their school bus. Two slept on the main floor and three had a room downstairs. Every time I passed the downstairs' doorway I would yell, "Hurry up or you'll miss your bus." I went back into my bedroom and called the doctor's office. They said I could come right over. I heard the boys scurrying out the door to catch their bus. As I passed through the kitchen I noticed that Tim had forgotten his lunch. That wasn't a major problem since I could drop his lunch off at his school on the way to the doctor's.

When I pulled into the school parking lot, two boys from his class were walking toward the entrance. I rolled down the car window and asked them to please give the lunch to Tim.

The doctor informed me the rash was from aspirin poisoning as I had just recovered from a viral infection the week before. I then drove to my school an hour late for work.

In the meantime the two classmates gave Tim's teacher his lunch. Since Tim was absent, she smelled a rat! She went to the other McLaughlin classrooms and pulled the brothers out of class. She demanded to know where he was. They didn't know. All they knew was he missed the bus. She wasn't buying that since Mom brought his lunch to school. She was convinced that he had skipped school.

Meanwhile, back at my desk, the phone rang and a little, tearful voice said, "Mom, I just woke up and I've missed my bus." I had a very understanding boss who allowed me to go home, pick up Tim and drive him to school. I dropped him off at the entrance and returned to work. Tim walked into his

23

classroom and the teacher said, "Well, where have you been Mr. McLaughlin?" He told her what happened. Of course, she didn't believe his mother brought him to school when his mother brought his lunch to school two hours earlier.

I couldn't believe my stupid rash could cause so much confusion to my family, Tim's school and my employer.

This brings to mind the time Tim really did skip school. He was a senior in high school when he informed me, "Tomorrow is Senior Skip Day." I assured him he would get into trouble and probably wouldn't graduate. "Everybody in the whole senior class is skipping school tomorrow" I was told. I reminded him that they always say they will but never do. As it turned out, Tim and his three best friends were the only four out of a hundred seniors that skipped school that day.

12. IT'S A MATCH

When Jeff graduated from the 8th Grade at St. Louis, graduation ceremonies were held in the parish church. Following the graduation everyone was invited to the school auditorium for refreshments.

After chatting with other parents for a while I was dying for a cigarette. I got one out of my purse but couldn't find a match. I glanced around the auditorium searching for someone smoking so I could borrow a match. I finally spotted a man leaning against the stage with a lit cigarette in his mouth. I sashayed up to him and asked him for a match. Much to my horror, the man suffered from multiple sclerosis. He immediately started hitting himself in the chest in an effort to reach his matches in his shirt pocket. I just wanted to die. I was too embarrassed to reach into his pocket and grab the matches and too polite to just walk away and leave him groping with his arm while leaning on the stage to hold his legs up. Our Father was watching this from a distance. He looked down at his sons and said, "If this doesn't make her quit smoking, nothing will!

13. SNEAKER SQUEAKER

Our property adapted well to picnics, parties, etc., for large groups since we had two acres. Our Father erected a basketball court on the patio, a baseball diamond with backstop, volleyball, and eventually a pool. We also had the ponies. Keith always resented the fact that when we had parties he had to give all the kiddies' pony rides. That really put a damper on his playtime.

We had a family reunion and my mother-in-law stayed overnight so I could take her to the Columbia Mall the following day. Everyone was ready to go to the mall but Tim couldn't find his sneakers. We all joined in the search to no avail. He insisted they were gone and I insisted that they were wherever he had removed them. He obviously couldn't go to the mall barefoot and Grandma Mac was getting impatient. I finally had to announce that he would have to stay at home. The tears started flowing. I felt bad but we all got in the car and left him screaming and crying in the driveway. To this day I still feel guilty about leaving him home that day.

A week later we received a package in the mail from my sister-in-law in Virginia. It was none other than Tim's sneakers. Her son had taken them home by mistake.

14. OBSCENE PHONE CALLS

While I was cleaning the kitchen after dinner and Our Father was mowing the lawn, the phone rang. The boys were scattered. A gentleman asked if it was the McLaughlin residence. When I answered, "Yes" he said, "It is?" He then asked if Keith lived there. After I answered him he said in a bewildered voice, "He does?" He inquired if we lived on Garden Road and followed up with, "You do?" Then he dropped the bombshell. He said he had been receiving obscene phone calls on his telephone answering machine. "I realize now that your son obviously isn't involved but it must be someone that your son is acquainted with," he admitted. He volunteered to playback the obscene phone calls for me to hear. I was afraid he was a pervert so I suggested he play the calls back for my husband and told him I would have him call him back.

Our Father returned his call with me listening in on the extension. The man ran through his story again and played back the obscene message. A voice that I didn't recognize said, "Hi, I'm Keith McLaughlin, I live at 9000 Garden Road. My phone number is 804-5555, Go F--- yourself." I couldn't believe my ears. My mind was racing trying to figure out what despicable kid would do such a thing to my angelic son. The man broke my concentration by adding, "Oh, there's more. Listen to this one." The message was, "Erase that last call but go F--- yourself anyway." I was horrified. The voice was unmistakably that of our son, Tim. Can you imagine what it's like for a Mother to hear her own son uttering such a thing over the telephone? I pulled myself together and ran to the other phone where Our Father was standing, equally in shock. He assured the man that he didn't recognize any of the voices but he would certainly check into it for him and call him back.

When Tim, Dennis and Keith returned home Our Father

called a family meeting. He recounted the phone call from a man who was receiving obscene phone calls. They knew nothing about any obscene phone calls. Absolutely nothing. Our Father mentioned that the man played back the messages for us and we recognized one of the voices. Suddenly, they did remember something about some obscene phone calls. It seems they didn't have school that day but Mom had to work. I trusted them. They were 11, 12 and 13 and old enough, I thought, to stay home alone and not invite any friends over.

This is the revised version of the story. Two friends happened to stop by. One of them had the phone number of a man who had this new answering machine. One of the friends called the number and compromised Keith. Tim was afraid they might get into trouble so he made the second call in hopes that the man was a total idiot and would erase the first call.

Our Father called the fathers of the other two boys and invited them all over for a tête-à-tête in our living room. By the time Our Father unloaded the tale to the other two fathers, the five culprits were scared shitless. We were pretty well convinced that there would be no further obscene phone calls from our telephone after Our Father told them they could go to jail for doing it.

The following day Our Father called the man and told him he didn't know who was responsible but he was quite sure he wouldn't get any more calls because word was getting around that Our Father was hot on their trail. The man was relieved and thanked Our Father for his cooperation in the matter.

15. HORSEPLAY

With the arrival of Twinkles we were encouraged to let Jeff and Kevin join the 4-H Hi-Riders Club. I was a little apprehensive because most of the members were in their teens and my boys were nine and eleven. We invited the Hi-Riders to have a meeting at our house so we could observe first hand whether or not we wanted them to become members of the club. I can't tell you how impressed we were with the conduct of these young people. They bent over backwards to share their knowledge of horses and horsemanship with the younger kids. Needless to say, they joined the Hi-Riders.

Before long we had two ponies. The newer edition was named Smokey. Smokey had a mind of his own. Every time Kevin got on that pony he would try to throw him off. His front legs would go up three times. If that didn't throw him, the hind legs would go up three times. Smokey had to do this at least 15 times before he would give up and go where Kevin wanted him to go.

The boys would go on overnight trail rides with the Hi-Riders. Eventually they were entering horse shows. After a couple of years, Jeff saved enough money cutting a neighbor's grass to buy a horse. About this time they started a younger club called the Lo-Riders and Tim, Dennis and Keith joined that.

We read in the paper that they were going to have a horse auction at the Howard County Fairgrounds. Jeff bought a black horse that he named Flanagan and a leather saddle. Flanagan wasn't in the best of shape when Jeff bought him but he had a lot of potential, according to his 4-H leader. When we got him home we realized he was covered with lice and had to be deloused. He had been gelded but apparently Flanagan didn't know what that meant.

Jeff worked and worked with Flanagan and before long his coat was shining and he was ready for the horse shows. Jeff managed to win some ribbons with Flanagan but not without frustration. Jeff would parade him around the ring while the judge carefully evaluated each horse and rider. However, if there was a mare in heat in the ring, Flanagan would take off lickety-split across the middle of the ring to the mare, disqualifying Jeff. In fact, if there was a mare in heat anywhere within five miles of our house, Flanagan would jump the fence and takeoff for the mare. We got many calls at 2:00 and 3:00 in the morning, "Would you please come get your damn horse." One night Our Father was so mad he tied Flanagan to his rear bumper and drove home as fast as he could with Flanagan trying desperately to keep pace with the truck.

We were watching TV one cold winter night. We heard a loud clopping sound in the basement. CLOP, CLOP, CLOP! Our Father went to see what was going on. Keith was in the house with two horses. Our Father, trying to control himself, asked, "What in the world are you doing?" He responded, "Dad, the weatherman said it's going to get really cold tonight and we have to bring all of our animals in the house!"

Jeff's best friend, Tommy, came from a large family. His father was our Veterinarian. One day at the dinner table, Jeff asked, "Mom, did you know that Mrs. Lewis is going to have another baby?" Keith, who was six, responded, "Shucks, I didn't even know Mrs. Lewis was in heat!"

The first day of summer vacation was always very special. It meant I could go shopping and not have to rush. Of course, I had to take the whole family with me but I didn't have to hurry. It was wonderful. I finished grocery shopping. We went to lunch at McDonald's and I even had time to browse through Kresge's.

Several 4-H members met us as we turned into our driveway. They were bubbling over with excitement. Our horse, Irish, had fallen into a perk hole. Now this wasn't your every day perk hole. It was the size of a grave and about eight feet deep. The boys had permission to graze their horses on adjacent acreage that was about to be developed.

We hurried across the field and found about fifteen people

peering into the perk hole. Irish was standing there on all fours down in the pit. The 4-Hers had called the police who told them to try the fire department who told them to phone the Animal Control Officer. The Animal Control Officer was at a complete loss as to what to do. He advised me to call a tow truck. I ran back home and called the tow truck. I wondered if our car insurance would pay for the tow truck. It took about twenty minutes for the tow truck to respond only to learn that the weight of the horse might pull the truck into the hole. The Animal Control Officer, as a last resort, decided the only way to get him out of the hole was with the State Police helicopter. That did it. No way were we paying for a helicopter.

I ran home and called Our Father. I was in tears as I blurted out the news. Our Father said, "Calm down and call John and ask him to bring his backhoe over and dig him out." It took an hour but John arrived and dug poor Irish out of the perk hole. When he got a ramp dug out for him to walk up, Irish refused to move. Finally, one of the older Hi-Riders jumped into the hole and led Irish up the ramp. So much for summer vacation and that was only the first day.

16. CORVAIR DESPAIR

Occasionally Our Father and his co-workers would go to Pope's Creek after work to eat crabs. The boys were asleep and I was watching a movie on TV when he returned home. He told me that the fan belt broke on the Corvair about five miles from home but since no gas stations were open he drove it home anyway. He also said the car was smoking a little so he didn't park in the carport. He parked in the driveway.

I was only half listening because I was engrossed in the movie. The pilot and co-pilot were both dead and Doris Day was attempting to land the plane herself. Suddenly I noticed brightness through the drapes. I pulled them open and saw flames shooting out of the car. Our Father ran outside and I ran to call the Fire Department. I awoke the boys and we joined Our Father at the bonfire.

When told that I had called the Fire Department, Our Father asked, "What did you do that for? The car is gone." I said, "Because the first question the insurance company is going to ask is, 'Did you call the Fire Department?'." He then informed me that we didn't have fire insurance coverage on the Corvair.

We invited the firemen into the house for a cup of coffee when there was nothing left but a skeleton in the driveway. It was then that it dawned on us that we would still be making car payments for one more year.

17. DAMP CAMP

Our sons were registered for 4-H camp in the mountains of Western Maryland in 1972. I made a special request. Since the boys were always together they had a tendency to be clannish. I asked that they be separated into different tribes.

The night before they left I walked past Keith's room and he was sitting on his bed weeping. I put my arms around him and tried to console him. He didn't want to go. I was really shocked because he was going to be with his brothers. I finally convinced him he was going to have a wonderful time and would love camping. I didn't sleep well because I was afraid it was an omen and that something terrible was going to happen. It was the first time that they were going to be separated from us.

The next day we drove them to the Fairgrounds and helped them board the bus. On the way home I started having stomach pangs. How could I ever have let them go away together without Our Father and me to watch over them? I knew it was a dreadful mistake.

Two days later Hurricane Agnes hit Maryland. I was so happy the boys were in the mountains because they were on high ground. We lived a mile from the Patuxent River that is controlled by Brighton Dam (a few miles away). Our road always flooded when they opened up the floodgates but we lived on higher ground. This Hurricane was apparently too much for Brighton Dam. The officials were afraid the Dam would break. Around 2:00 A.M. the fire department using loud speakers advised everyone to evacuate their homes. This was almost more than I could bear. I was separated from my babies and now I might lose my home.

Our Father refused to evacuate. He had seen the water tables for our area and was convinced we were too high to be affected by the dam breaking. So we stayed. The following morning the radio reported flooding in the mountains of Western Maryland. Now I was spastic. There was no way to get in touch with our family. We just had to wait it out and pray.

The storm subsided, the dam didn't break, and it was finally time to meet the bus at the fairgrounds. I was a nervous wreck. We waited and waited for two and a half hours. Just when I was sure I would never see my family again the bus arrived. They were late because so many of the mountain roads were closed due to the flooding.

The boys were filled with exciting camping tales, pranks, etc. When I asked if they were all in different cabins, Keith replied, "No, we were all together." So much for separating the clannish McLaughlins.

18. STATIC CLING

Our Father came home from work one evening and I immediately sensed he wasn't a happy camper. He greeted me with, "From now on you will hand wash and hand iron all of my shirts." To say that I was stunned would be an understatement considering that I worked all day, prepared dinner for seven, cleaned and did laundry whether I wanted to or not. I, of course, asked the logical question, "Why?"

That day he had given a seminar to a group of supervisors. He used a chalkboard for his demonstration. Every time he turned around to the blackboard, he detected snickers coming from the group. When he faced them they would be quite straight faced. After this happened several times, someone tapped him on the back and informed him that a pair of nylon panties were hanging off the back of his shirt.

When he finished his recitation he threw my crumpled up panties on the kitchen counter.

My response was, "You think you're embarrassed. How the hell do you think I feel?" They definitely were not my Sunday go to Meeting panties!

19. BLOCKING OUT

One of the ways I survived raising five sons, especially five teenagers, was my method of "blocking them out." Five boys in one room can make a lot of noise. To keep my sanity, I got to the point where I could tune out the noise and do my own thing. There were times when the house was vibrating from loud music but I was able to carry on by tuning it out. Our Father never learned the technique. There were times, however, when "blocking out" didn't work to my advantage.

One summer morning the boys left the house on their bicycles. I was standing at the sink doing dishes when shortly Tim returned home. He said, "Do you know where the Brown's house is?" I said, "Yes." "Do you know where Mink Hollow Road and Deer Valley Road meet?" "Yes." It took Tim a long time to get to the point so I tuned him out and went on doing my dishes. He went on for five minutes with his directions before I heard, "And there's blood all over the street." "Blood all over the street," I yelled, "Where?" And then he said, "Do you know where the Brown's live?" I jumped in the car and sped to the Brown's house where I found Jeff lying on the street with his knee gaping open and Kevin, Dennis and Keith helplessly standing over him. Why they didn't just knock on the Brown's door, I will never know. It took Tim at least ten minutes to come back home and another five minutes before I realized Jeff had fallen off his bike.

Another example of bad blocking out occurred when they were in their teens. When I got home from work I would gather up the mail and newspaper, fix myself a glass of sherry and quietly relax. It was my reward for working all day. Jeff came in the kitchen door where I was sitting with my nose in the newspaper. He had an after school job milking cows at a nearby dairy farm. He said, "I had a bad day. I was attacked by a bull." I said, "Uh huh," and kept on reading. He went on for five minutes with things like, "I always liked Charlie. I don't know why Charlie turned on me." I glanced up over the paper and almost fell on the floor. Jeff was standing there with his clothes in shreds, his hat was on sideways and he was covered with cuts and scratches.

Charlie, the bull, had indeed turned on him. Jeff said he threw him up in the air with his horns and he landed up against the fence. He couldn't get away because Charlie had him cornered. Jeff said Charlie would put his head down, move his front feet back and forth, snort and come after him again and again. He finally realized he wasn't getting out of there alive and mustered up enough strength to hoist himself up and over the fence. Did I mention he was wearing his red Exxon jacket that day? I know it sounds like a lot of bull but it really happened.

20. BIKE STRIKE

My friend's husband was a manufacturer's representative
for a line of women's clothing. In the Spring he would show
his fall line to the buyers from the better stores. In the fall he
would show his spring and cruise wear. When he presented a
new line his previous samples would become obsolete. He
would sell them to us for wholesale prices. Occasionally, he
would bring racks and racks of dresses and sportswear to my
house. I would invite all of my friends and coworkers over to
sort through, try on and eventually purchase these bargains.
Since they were in my home I had the advantage of trying on
everything and, believe me, I did.

I remember I was in between outfits, half naked, when the
phone rang. It was Keith. "Mom, you better come quick.
Tim's been hit by a car down by the bridge." I ran to the door
to call Our Father who was swimming. Every time I yelled his
name he would go under water. I frantically tried to get my
clothes on while yelling for him at the same time. He finally
heard my pleas and came running but he had to get dressed
also. It was only minutes but it seemed like an hour before we
were in the car on our way to the scene.

A friend of the boys had been hit by a car while riding his
bike the week before. It bent his bike a little but, fortunately,
he wasn't hurt. I guess I had this in the back of my mind
because I was totally unprepared for what I found. He was
laying in the middle of the road. A neighbor had covered him
with a blanket and was crouched over him. He was conscious
but his face was so swollen he was unrecognizable. There was
no indentation around his nose and since he had broken blood
vessels in his eyes they were blood red. Our Father pulled
down the blanket. His left leg was laying toward the street as
if it were detached from his body. All the skin was torn off his
right leg and ankle. I still have a hard time believing it but a
man came up to me and said, "Lady, if you think he looks bad,

38

you should see the car."

According to the driver, as he approached the bridge Keith came out of a side road on his bike, followed by Dennis. As the driver swerved to miss Dennis, Tim came flying into the intersection and he hit him broadside. Tim flew up into the windshield, breaking it with his right arm and leg as he went through it. When the driver was finally able to stop the car, Tim was thrown thirty feet into the air before landing on the blacktop.

The ambulance finally arrived and they secured him in the back. I climbed in to accompany him to the hospital, I thought, but the ambulance wouldn't start. Our Father wanted to transfer him into our station wagon and transport him because we were losing valuable time. The rescue squad wouldn't hear of it. They called for another ambulance from an adjacent county. It was another ten or fifteen minutes before they responded.

When he came out of surgery he had a fractured femur, knee and tibia on his left leg and multiple cuts on his right arm. His right leg was in a cast. They put a steel pin through his knee to hold the left leg in traction for three months. To put it mildly, he was a mess.

We didn't arrive back home until late Saturday night. I had forgotten that I had invited numerous friends to my clothing party. My neighbor, Becky, who was my biggest buyer anyway, had taken over completely in my absence. I spent all day Sunday at the hospital while Becky greeted the bargain hunters for me.

I would spend all day at the hospital and leave in time to come home and fix dinner for Our Father and the brothers. The phone rang off the hook with concerned friends calling. I was trying to prepare a meal and talk on the phone when the operator broke into the line and told me to hang up and wait for an emergency call. All I could think of was that Tim had taken a turn for the worse. I couldn't even answer the phone when it rang. Our Father answered it and found out that Kevin had an accident in our station wagon about two miles away. He wasn't hurt but the car, which I needed desperately, was. When we arrived at the scene, the man who had phoned us was elated to see that we had so many sons. He was a little league football coach for St. Peter's and he needed players.

Tim's hospitalization put a dent in all of our lives. Keith was playing little league football but in an entirely different direction than the hospital. Since I spent all day with Tim I couldn't carpool him to football. After dinner I would return to the hospital with Our Father after stopping at Roy Rogers and getting Tim a cheeseburger, fries and vanilla shake every day for three months. He refused to eat hospital food.

St. Peter's was directly across the street from the hospital. Keith joined St. Peter's football team. We dropped him off on the way to the hospital and picked him up on the way home. With my car out of commission, Our Father received special permission to bring a company car home and I drove Our Father's car.

When school started, Tim, who was a sophomore, had to have special tutors come to the hospital every day. He finally came home from the hospital in November. He had an orthopedic leg brace so he couldn't return to school until the second semester. The tutors continued teaching him at home.

Keith's original little league team did so well that year that they won a trip to Orlando to play in a bowl game. That went over like a lead balloon. He didn't blame me though. He blamed Tim!

21. DEEP CREEK LAKE

In 1961 we took the boys to Nags Head for a week. Because we all have fair skin we burned to a crisp the first day on the beach. Our Father wanted to try the mountains so in 1962 I solicited mountain vacation brochures. I mentioned this to our friend, Joan, at a crab feast and she insisted that we join her family and friends at Deep Creek Lake the last week in July. I had no idea what we were getting into but I made reservations at Railey's Cottages. Railey's had six stone cabins right on the lake. We were able to confirm cabin #6.

The cabins were small. We had a two bedroom with an open-out sofa. The living area consisted of a stone fireplace, an oak ball and claw foot table, four chairs and a dinky kitchen area. By the time we set up the playpen, port-a-crib, and luggage for seven people, we could hardly move around.

Joan had told me to bring summer and winter clothing because it can get very cold in the mountains. She also told us to bring our own beer because it's very expensive at the lake. I remember Kevin asking, "Why are there four cases of beer for two people and only one case of Cokes for five?" I told him to mind his own business, drove to the store and bought one more case of Cokes. Keith was nine months old which meant we had three in diapers and they hadn't invented disposable ones. There was no washer or dryer at Railey's. By the time I finished packing changes of clothing for seven (winter and summer), diapers, food, beer, crib, etc., we needed a Greyhound bus just to get there.

Railey's had a large floating dock. We spent all day sitting on the dock unless we were on a boat. The children weren't allowed near the lake without their life preservers on. We had twenty children among us, all wearing orange "servers." They were the only ones that would venture into the water since the lake was so cold. The adults did water ski but for the most part we sat on the dock all bundled up.

41

At night we built a campfire and the children would roast marshmallows until bedtime. After they were asleep the adults would gather around the campfire, drink beer, snack and tell jokes. My sides would ache from laughing so hard. We could never figure out why God made us hurt from laughing.

Two childless couples shared cabin #1. They were the envy of the Railey bunch. Every evening they would dress up, take their boat and go to a lakeside restaurant for dinner while we slaved over the stove.

Since it was our first trip we were told we had to visit Swallow Falls. It was always cold in the morning so we dressed the boys in sweaters, long pants and hiking boots (and booties). When we got back to the compound the minipoos (as we called them) were all in the water with their servers on and our friends were just beginning to get motivated for the day.

We were talking about our adventuresome trip to the falls when Jack came running out of his cabin, right through the crowd and jumped into the lake with all of his clothes on. We thought he was showing off and got a huge laugh out of his antics until he pulled Dennis out of the lake, hiking boots and all. There were thirteen adults standing there and not one of us noticed Dennis standing on the dock without his server on. Jack was sitting at his oak table drinking a cup coffee and, Thank God, saw him fall into the lake. We learned a valuable lesson that day.

Maybe you had to be there but the funniest things happened at Deep Creek Lake during the twenty years we vacationed there. I shall try to relate some of them but not necessarily in chronological order.

Our friend, Ed, had received a promotion in the insurance field. He wanted to take us all out and buy us a beer to celebrate. Since no one could recall Ed ever treating anyone to a beer, we were all determined to go. Some spouses had to remain at the campfire lest there be a whimper from one of the cabins but most of the crowd boarded boats for the excursion. We embarked at The Cellar Door, a nearby lakeside bar. There was only one table occupied that evening so we all sat at the bar.

Ed proudly ordered a round of Budweiser for everyone at the bar. While sipping our beer we tried to figure out how we were going to retaliate. Someone noticed some small 6 oz. bottles of beer on the shelf. It was Rolling Rock, a Pennsylvania beer that none of us had ever heard of. When our Budweisers were empty someone ordered a round of 6 oz. Rolling Rocks. Ed just shook his head in disbelief. One of the men at the only occupied table yelled out, "Don't tell me you're drinking that stuff. It tastes like the bottom of a birdcage." Well, that just made it perfect for our payback to Ed. We had hardly begun drinking the Rolling Rock when the bartender set us up with another round. The bartender told us the man at the table was the local distributor for Rolling Rock and he was so pleased that we bought his beer that he bought us a round.

All of the piers and docks at Deep Creek are floating so that they can be pulled out of the lake in the winter. It's hard to keep your balance on floating piers especially when there are a lot of people walking on it. When we left The Cellar Door that night and were walking on the pier, Gube fell in the lake. What made it even funnier was the fact that he came out of the lake faster than he went in. We laughed all the way back to the campfire.

There were other paybacks, too. One of the childless couples finally adopted two children and bingo before long they had two of their own. They were saddled with four minipoos. By then, all of our boys were teens and we would all get in the boats and take off for dinner while Liz slaved over the stove.

One night all of the adults went out together to the Pizza Pub. Our son, Tim, was thirteen so he baby-sat for the Bohne's four minipoos. We came sailing down the lake around midnight with everyone singing, "Roll Me Over in the Clover." We pulled up to the dock and were horrified to find the Bohne minipoos standing on there. Where was Tim? He was asleep in their cabin.

The kids always had to make many trips to the Trading Post that was about the only store on the lake. They would buy cigarette loads, smoke bombs and fake vomit--anything

43

they could get their hands on to trick people. I was almost afraid to smoke at the lake for fear my cigarette would explode.

One rainy day all the adults gathered in one cabin to play cards while the kids all gathered in another cabin. When our friend, Russ, who is a born comedian realized what was going on he took one of the boys. He wrapped both of his arms in bandages and poured ketchup all over him. Then he came running into the adult cabin with Matt in his arms yelling, "I just went over to the sawmill and found Matt...." All of the mothers were in a state of panic. Some started running toward the sawmill before realizing it was a joke.

Another rainy day the kids all came running out of their cabin screaming, "The cabin is on fire." It seems the McLaughlin boys had climbed up on the roof and dropped smoke bombs down the chimney into the fireplace. The smell was just starting to dissipate by the time we checked out on Saturday.

22. HAIRCUT REBELLIONS

Our Father has had a crew cut for as long as I have known him. It seemed only natural that his five sons would follow in his footsteps. Tim was our first son born with hair that had body. His hair actually curled. It was beautiful. I returned home from Mass on Sunday morning when Tim was six months old and found my beautiful, curly haired son with a crew cut. That's when I realized there wasn't any choice in the matter.

Good friends of ours adopted a child. It took years of waiting and red tape but it was well worth it. He was adorable and his head was covered with auburn locks. The adoption agency made periodic visits to their home to be sure Tommy was being properly cared for. Our friends called one Sunday. The adoption agency was coming for inspection the following day and Tommy needed a haircut. Would Our Father please cut his hair? Tommy didn't have a crew cut and Our Father wasn't adept at state of the art coiffing but he, of course, complied with the request. If his hair hadn't been dark red it wouldn't have been so noticeable. Our boys were all towheads so mistakes were hardly recognizable. When Our Father put down his clippers we were all speechless. Our friends didn't sleep that night. They had visions that the agency would take away their long awaited child.

Our Father acquired a telephone operator's chair at an auction and eventually he would set up shop in the basement. You could raise and lower the chair and even spin it. They would line up and Our Father would zap that hair right off their heads. That worked well until the Beatles hit the music scene and changed the world.

That's when the problems started. Our sons, especially the older ones, wanted longer hair. Our Father didn't like the Beatles or their music and his sons certainly weren't going to look like them. Those happy haircut days of yore were gone

45

forever. They became tearful ordeals that lasted all day.

Things really got bad when Jeff was a senior in high school. They made me the hair go-between. Our Father would issue an order before he left for work. "You tell Jeff to get a haircut before I get home from work." I would obediently pass on the message but would be told, "I'm old enough to wear my hair any way I want to. You tell Dad I'm not getting a haircut." I felt as if I was on "the rack" being pulled in different directions. "You tell Jeff he's not living in this house unless he gets a haircut." "You tell Dad I have no intention of getting my hair cut."

Finally I put my foot down and announced, "No child will be put out of this house until they graduate from high school." I dreaded Jeff's graduation day because he still hadn't been to the barber and I knew what was coming. His friends nicknamed him "Locks." The day after graduation the ultimatum was issued. I was a wreck. My stomach was all tied up in knots. I approached Jeff and informed him he would have to get a haircut or move out of the house. He replied, "You can't put me out of this house. This is my house. I live here and I'm not leaving." I was never so relieved in my life!

Before Beatles.

After Beatles.

23. VALIANT WASN'T A PRINCE

When my aunt was pushing eighty she decided she wouldn't renew her driver's license and would sell her Valiant. She had parked it for years on a side street next to her apartment in D.C. There wasn't a part of the car that wasn't dented or scratched. We decided it would be a perfect car for our sons and bought it from her. It looked bad but ran good. Perfect transportation to school and work.

Jeff was working at Centennial High School at the time. The first call I got was from Centennial High. "Mom, I fell off the roof of the auditorium but I don't think I'm hurt, just shaken up a bit."

The second call was from the Howard County Police Department. The officer told me that my Plymouth was abandoned on Folly Quarter Road and because it was on the crest of a hill it could cause an accident. I was told to remove it immediately. I protested, "Officer, I don't own a Plymouth." He assured me that I did. He said it was registered to Harry B. and Helen M. McLaughlin. "That's impossible," I said, "We have never owned a Plymouth in our life." He replied, "Lady, you own a Plymouth Valiant and it's obstructing traffic and you better get it out of there." Why didn't he say it was a Valiant in the first place?

Our sons all went to Our Lady of Good Counsel High School about fifteen miles from our home. Our Father dropped them off on his way to work in D.C. and picked them up on his way home. They always had football, basketball, wrestling practice or detention after school anyway. One day my car wouldn't start after work. Someone got it started and told me not to stop until I got home because it would never start again. I was elated that it made it home.

Dennis called from school and asked me to pick him up because he couldn't wait for Dad. I explained that my car had died and he insisted that I drive the Valiant. That Valiant was a thorn in my side. Nothing worked on it. The speedometer was broken, the gas gauge didn't work. To top it off one of the boys had lost the gas cap and they had a sweatsock stuffed in the hole. I always have been a nervous driver. I wouldn't drive on the Beltway if my life depended on it. Just the thought of driving in traffic immediately gives me diarrhea. To pick up Dennis at school meant advanced diarrhea.

I was driving on Layhill Road, a very hilly road, and halfway there when the car unexpectedly lost power. I was on the top of a hill and could see a gas station near the bottom. I knew if I could coast that far I'd be saved. I coasted right up to the pump. The only problem was I was at the "do it yourself" pump and I was the "full service" type. I went over to the young attendant and explained that I was out of gas and begged him to put gas in my car. Then I had to endure the humiliation of the sweatsock. My boys never put more than a dollar's worth of gas in the car at one time because one of their brothers might use some of their gas.

I finally reached Georgia Avenue. Georgia Avenue has six lanes of traffic and I would have to make a U turn to pick him up in front of school. As I approached the school I couldn't believe my eyes. He was standing there hitchhiking. I rolled down my window and screamed out his name across three lanes of traffic to no avail. As I made my U turn I saw him get into a car and speed off up Georgia Avenue. I could have strangled him. Then I began to worry that the person who picked him up might molest him or kidnap him. I had diarrhea for a week!

24. GRADUATIONLESS

Jeff couldn't rent a normal tuxedo for his senior prom. He had to go to downtown D.C. and rent a gold lame tuxedo with a gold top hat for the occasion. Unfortunately, he couldn't pick it up until the afternoon of the prom. You didn't have to be a mathematician to figure out there was no way he could pick up the tuxedo after school in D.C., drive all the way home, change, pick up his date and arrive at the pre-prom dinner on time. So he did what he said any red blooded American boy would do. He skipped study hall, picked up his tux and returned in time for his next class. There was one major problem. He got caught.

We were notified that he may not graduate because of breaking this school rule. Outside of throwing food across the cafeteria when he was a freshman, he had never been in trouble before (that we knew of) and now he wasn't going to graduate. That boggled my mind. We sat at his graduation with our fingers crossed until his name was called out.

Kevin managed to get through four years of high school without any problems until the dreaded notification arrived. Kevin was failing Algebra II. The same damn thing happened. We went to the graduation and sweated it out until his name was finally called.

Tim breezed through four years with no problems until Senior Skip Day. The four Skippers were told they were not graduating unless they could come up with a note from a parent stating that they were really sick that day. I looked at Our Father and said, "I absolutely refuse to go through another graduationless graduation. Give me the paper and pen!" I even mentioned I had to take him to the doctors. Tim came home from school with a wide smile on his face. The Principal rejected the other Skippers notes but accepted Tim's because "Your mother would never tell a lie!" I felt like two cents but damn if I didn't enjoy that graduation.

50

25. ACCIDENTS WILL HAPPEN

Our Father decided he wanted an old classic Chris Craft
boat. Tim was visiting Deep Creek Lake and found two old
Chris Crafts for sale at a marina there. We decided to make
the trip and check out the boats. The boat that Our Father
liked was in the water but they were doing some work on it
because it had a fuel leak. The owner said we could try it out
but we would have to leave the motor cover off so gas fumes
could escape.

We took skis with us so we could test how it would do
towing skiers. Kevin and Keith accompanied us. We gave it a
good trial run with both boys skiing. Everyone took turns at
the wheel. When it was time for Keith at the helm, Kevin got
out of the seat and backed up for Keith to sit down. In doing
so he backed his left heel into the flywheel on the motor. It cut
through his heel like a chainsaw. Our Father grabbed his foot
and held the heel together and shouted to Keith, "Step on it!"
Kevin only had one leg to stand on and the speed of the boat
was making it almost impossible for Kevin and Our Father to
balance themselves. I kept yelling, "Slow down" but Our
Father outdid me with, "Go faster!".

When we got back to the dock a woman handed me a brand
new beach towel to wrap around his foot. I protested because
blood was everywhere but she insisted. They carried Kevin to
the car and we sped to the hospital in Oakland, Maryland. We
returned home with Kevin, two crutches and a classic Chris
Craft.

The boating accident happened in June but the heel stitches
wouldn't heal. Two weeks later Kevin (still on crutches) and
Tim were driving home in Kevin's van when they had a head-
on collision with a truck two miles from our home. Our
Father was swimming and I was catching rays on the chaise
when our neighbor, Jeff, ran up our driveway yelling, "You

better come quick. Kevin and Tim were in an accident at the end of Mink Hollow Road. Kevin's okay but they put Tim in an ambulance. You can't use Mink Hollow because the police have it blocked off."

Our Father opted to go to the scene and sent me to the hospital with our neighbor. The only way to get there without using Mink Hollow was five miles longer. It was the longest ride of my life. I didn't know what I was going to find when I got to the hospital and I didn't think we were ever going to get to the hospital. I waited frantically in the emergency room and finally Our Father and Kevin arrived, followed shortly by Jeff, Dennis and Keith. Kevin said the police were sure he was hurt because he was standing at the scene on crutches.

After what seemed like an eternity, the doctor came out to talk to us. He informed us our son had a broken jaw (all of his teeth were knocked out) and a fractured right foot. Our Father referred to it as "hoof and mouth disease!" He would be having surgery in the morning with an oral surgeon working on the top and an orthopedic doctor working on the bottom simultaneously. He let me go in to see him. It broke my heart to see him in such pain. I told him I wish I could trade places with him. He couldn't open his mouth but he managed to mumble, "No you don't!"

I asked the oral surgeon after the operation how he could possibly put all of those teeth back in his mouth and have them stay. He said it was very easy. He just laid them all out on a tray in the right order and put them back in his gums. He told me some of them might not take but he was reasonably sure they would. Tim returned from surgery with his mouth wired shut and a cast on his right leg. How do you fill up an eighteen year old football player with liquids?

Two nights later we all left the hospital after visiting Tim. Kevin went home, Dennis and Keith went to a party and Our Father and I went to K-Mart. I had to buy one pair of sandals. The left one was for Tim to wear home from the hospital and the right one was for Kevin. We arrived home and Kevin told us that Dennis had called and that he had hit a man on a motorcycle on Muncaster Mill Road on his way to the party. I stood speechless while Our Father jumped into the car and headed for Muncaster Mill Road. The accident happened at dusk while Dennis was making a left turn at an intersection. He never saw the motorcyclist until he flipped into the air losing his helmet and shoes before landing. He was taken to the hospital while Our Father made arrangements to have Dennis' car towed home to join Kevin's totaled van in our driveway.

Later that night a nurse informed Tim he was getting a roommate. Tim asked who it was. She said it was a motorcycle accident victim. Tim said, "I don't think it's a good idea to put him in my room because my brother is the person who hit him." They quickly moved him to another room.

We were scheduled to go to Deep Creek Lake the following week. Tim was determined that he was not going with a cast on his leg and his mouth wired shut. Our Father and I discussed the situation and decided after what we had been through we desperately needed a change of scenery. Also taken into consideration was the fact that a large group of our friends were going and we could use a few laughs. After all, Tim was going to be miserable whether he was home or at the lake and the liquid diet was driving me to drink! The blender was on a 24-hour alert trying to satisfy his hunger.

We were staying at Alpine Village that year. Some of our friends were staying at Alpine and some were across the cove at Arrowhead. It was close enough that we could swim back and forth. After everyone arrived and everyone's boats were launched and docked, the adults got together for a much needed Cocktail Hour. Tim and his crutches and the other teens all gathered on the dock. The first report to hit the Cocktail Party was, "Tim has fallen overboard!" I really needed that! After dragging him out of the lake I was determined that we weren't going home, wet cast or no wet cast. We gathered together the hair dryers and proceeded to try to dry him out.

The next day Tim insisted on eating some French fries which he would force up between the wires. I was spasmodic for fear he would choke to death but he continued shoving them through the wires until he became unimmobilized. One thing for sure--I wasn't going home. I called his oral surgeon long distance and explained what had happened. He said he must be immobilized immediately. "If you can't find an oral surgeon that's familiar with this procedure, you'll have to bring him home." I told Our Father, "This is going to cost an arm and a leg but we're not going home." I phoned an oral surgeon in Oakland. He said he would go to the hospital, pick up what was needed and meet Tim at his office in an hour. No problem! He fixed him right up and only charged $25.00.

Things were really going our way until the third day when Keith fell off his skis and the ski hit him in the nose and broke it. I was beginning to think that maybe we should go home. Our Father took him to the hospital in Oakland but they said it couldn't be set until the swelling subsided (approximately three days). I was at my wit's end so I called Tim's oral surgeon at home again. He couldn't believe all this was happening to the same family. He couldn't have been nicer. He said he would make an appointment with a plastic surgeon for Keith but we would have to return home on Friday morning. At this point, I couldn't wait to get home. Tim already had an appointment Friday morning with the oral surgeon and another appointment at 3:00 with the orthopedic surgeon so if the plastic surgeon could be worked in between, what more could I ask for? We departed Deep Creek on Thursday.

Friday was going to be a major problem since Kevin's van was totaled, Dennis' front end was totaled and Keith wasn't old enough to drive. We all had to leave at the same time since I was the only source of wheels in the house. It meant we had to leave at 7:30 a.m. to make our first stop at the nursery where Dennis worked. Then off to the oral surgeon for an 8:30 appointment. Next was the nose setting at 10:00. Keith hadn't come out of the recovery room so I had to leave him and take Tim to the orthopedic surgeon and leave him and return for Keith. Keith and I returned to pick up Tim and then swung by the nursery to pick up Dennis after work at 4:00. You never heard such grumblings from the brothers. Tim thought he should have been taken home after his first appointment and picked up for his second. Keith didn't think he should have to sit around all day in waiting rooms waiting for Tim.

The same procedure went into effect for the court appearances. Kevin's hearing for his accident was the same day as Dennis' but one was in the morning session and the other in the afternoon. We stayed at court all day because I wasn't making two trips. Tim had to go with us because there wasn't anyone at home to take care of him. You should have heard the grumblings that day.

Shortly thereafter, the Sheriff came to our door and issued a summons. We were being sued for One Million Dollars (real money) by the motorcyclist. That just about finished me!

I write a poem for our Christmas greeting every year. This is the poem we sent in 1977:

Helen went to Ireland for two weeks in the Spring.
Harry bought a '57 Chris Craft so he could "do his thing"!
We won a year's free tuition to Good Counsel in May.
Things were going pretty good – wouldn't you say?

Well, that's the end of the good news for the year.
Everything else is all downhill from here.
The summer of '77 ended not a moment too soon.
Kevin was on crutches from a boating accident in June.

Two head-on collisions in three days in July.
On the "Luck o' the Irish" we do not rely.
Tim in the hospital for ten days in great pain.
His liquid diet for two months almost drove us insane!

Kevin's van was totaled – but the payments linger on.
And we now have eleven cars on the driveway and lawn.
Dennis' accident didn't seem quite as extensive.
But the million dollar lawsuit seems a bit expensive!

We went to Deep Creek Lake to forget our woes.
Keith went water-skiing and broke his nose.
Jeff thought he had no reason for alarm.
Until he played football and broke his arm!

The cat died – leaving us with her babies.
The way things are going Duffy will catch rabies.
Harry split his head open under Kevin's car.
We really do think things have gone a little too far.

Please come visit – if you can find a place to park.
Our holiday spirit could use a little spark.
We're all looking forward to a Happy New Year.
And hope that your holidays are full of good cheer.

The McLaughlins

Dennis' Ford.

Kevin's van.

26. TRASH TALK

Tim and Dennis worked their way through college by working for Browning Ferris, Inc. (better known as B.F.I.). They worked all summer and were also able to work when they came home for the Christmas holidays. Friends would ask, "How can they stand collecting garbage all day?" I would answer, "Hey, they're making $9.00 an hour and all they can eat!" That would shut them up. One of the teachers at school excitedly told me, "Your son, Tim, is my trashman."

Tim was collecting trash in the back of a house while a lady was hanging clothes on the line. He recognized a Good Counsel High School jersey hanging there. He asked, "Does your son go to Good Counsel?" She replied, "Yes." Tim said, "I graduated from there." Tim said her jaw dropped two inches. He chuckled and returned to his truck.

27. CRASH COURSE

Tim and a friend were driving to Frostburg one December night when a car coming down the mountain hit them head on. Tim's passenger said the last thing he remembered before the crash was Tim saying, "Look at this asshole!" We got the call from the hospital in Cumberland around 11:00 p.m. We made arrangements to pick up the passenger's parents and arrived in Cumberland about 2:30 a.m. Tim suffered bruised ribs and cuts but was released. His passenger didn't fare as well. He had a broken leg and was admitted. The car was totaled. The person responsible for the accident had no insurance (the story of our life!).

When Tim was a student at Frostburg State University he lived in an apartment on Main Street. To say it was a fire trap is putting it mildly. I was watching the news on TV when they announced a runaway truck sailed down Main Street in Frostburg, hitting cars, buildings and crashing into a store before coming to a rest. I ran to the phone but all lines into Frostburg were busy. I'm sure every parent of every student was on the phone. I was frantic as usual. It took hours before Tim answered the phone and informed me the truck crashed into the store right next to his apartment building and the police and firemen wouldn't allow them to enter their apartment. A few more gray hairs arrived soon after that experience.

We spent a week visiting Jeff and Keith in Texas. When we returned home my station wagon wasn't sitting in the driveway where I had left it. Kevin had a truck and a car. It seems they were both out of gas so he used my car, fell asleep at the wheel, ran off the road and rolled it in a field. It was as flat as a pancake.

I then inherited his unsightly car. Nothing worked. The hood wouldn't open, the speedometer didn't work and there was no gas gauge. I deplored it. I came out of work one evening and it wouldn't start (which was no surprise). My boss jumped it and told me not to stop until I got to my driveway. Unfortunately, I had to stop for gas or I would not make it home. I got the gas and naturally the car wouldn't start. The attendant that came to help me only had one arm and instead of a hand there was a hook. I knew the hood wouldn't open. I took one look at the hood and the hook and said, "Why me, Lord?"

We attended Tim's graduation in Frostburg. Following graduation we would be moving all of his personal effects back home. His car had died in the apartment parking lot weeks before but Our Father was confident he could get it started so he could bring it home. WRONG! They finally decided we would have to push it all the way home. I'm talking about a hundred and fifty miles. I do not react well to stressful situations. All I do is shake and pray.

Our Father would push him all the way up to the top of the mountain and let him coast all the way down. Just engaging his back bumper with our front bumper was enough to give me whiplash. The prayers became more intensive with each mountain we approached. Tim's exhaust was emitting such thick black smoke that the other drivers on the highway were blinded for a half mile radius. Your son's graduation day is supposed to be a happy memory. It was one of the worse days of my life. I'm convinced my prayers are the only reason we made it home, much less alive. Again, I had diarrhea for a week.

Hell's pancake.

Tim's mountain car.

28.   SPRECHEN SIE DEUTSCH?

All through High School our sons never brought a girl home to dinner. When it finally happened I didn't know what to do. Dennis informed me he invited not one but two girls to dinner. I was having stuffed peppers but since I was in shock I ran to the store and bought steaks. This was a great occasion. Then he told me they were German and didn't speak English. He said Gitta understood English but Suzanne didn't.

It was my responsibility to entertain the girls at our pool while Tim and Dennis played basketball and totally ignored them. Gitta and Suzanne spoke German while I lay mute on the chaise lounge. Eventually Our Father arrived home from work. Gitta said something in German. She probably said, "It is Dennis' father." All I picked up on was the word farter. I immediately broke my silence and said, "You're right about that!"

Dinner was very entertaining. It was like eating in the United Nations cafeteria with Gitta translating everything into German for Suzanne.

A year later Gitta and Suzanne went to Spain on vacation. They sent Dennis a postcard. It read: "The weather is here. Wish you were beautiful!"

29. WET T-SHIRT

We decided to visit Jeff and Keith in Texas during Easter vacation, 1981. The week before we were scheduled to leave we received a phone call at 2:30 in the morning. When you have five sons and the phone rings in the middle of the night it's similar to being struck by lightning. It was Jeff. He said, "You're never going to believe this, Mom, but Kim just won a wet T-shirt contest. She was a finalist and tonight she won. She won a trip to Hawaii. The only problem is WE have to leave next week for Hawaii." I was crushed. I was really looking forward to our trip to Texas but we weren't going to drive fourteen hundred miles if we couldn't visit with both sons. The conversation continued. I asked, "Who is Kim?" He replied, "Oh, Kim is my new girlfriend and she just won a wet T-shirt contest. You do know what a wet T-shirt contest is, don't you, Mom?" I said, "Of course." As soon as I hung up the phone I said to Our Father, "What the hell is a wet T-shirt contest?" He didn't know either.

I found out the next day at work from one of the younger faculty members. To tell you the truth, I was a little shocked and even more upset that my trip to Dallas was canceled.

A year later I got another one of those calls. "Mom, you're never going to believe it but Kim is on the Centerfold in the May issue of Playboy." I couldn't wait to go to work with this report.

In the meantime, Our Father had a hernia operation. During his recuperation I got the word that the May issue of Playboy had hit the newsstands. There was no way in this world I was going into a store and ask the clerk for a copy of Playboy. Our Father couldn't drive, in fact he could hardly move, but he insisted I drive him to the store. He grimaced in pain as he dragged his body out of the car and into the store as he loudly proclaimed, "Do you have the May issue of

Playboy? My son's girlfriend is on the centerfold." I couldn't believe it. He was as proud as a peacock.

Jeff brought her to Deep Creek Lake to meet the family that summer. I realized immediately how she won the wet T-shirt contest. It's not that I'm all that perceptive, it's that Our Father once gave me a T-shirt that read, "In case of rape THIS SIDE UP!"

30. CAKE CAPER

Tim's birthday is July 30th. We always planned our
annual vacation for the last week in July. Consequently, we
were always able to celebrate Tim's birthday on vacation,
usually at Deep Creek Lake. When the boys got older they
didn't want to go on vacation with Mom and Dad anymore
Tim was in college and we were going to be in Nags Head for
a week. It would be the first time we wouldn't be with him on
his birthday.

How could a Mother not bake a birthday cake for her son?
The guilt trip was starting to build. The day before vacation
always caused me great stress -- so much to do--so little time.
Dennis passed me in the kitchen and on the way out the door
announced he was driving to Olney to get a part for his car.
The thought hit me out of nowhere. I ran to the door and
asked him to stop at Carvel's ice cream store and get me an ice
cream cake. This was wonderful. I could put it in the freezer
and on Tim's birthday I could call him and surprise him by
telling him to look in the freezer. Dennis, of course, declined.
It would take too long and he was in a big hurry. By now I
was begging. "Please, Dennis, it won't take you five minutes
to pick up the cake." He reluctantly agreed. I said, "Have
them write 'Happy Birthday Tim' on the cake." Well, that did
it. Now it was definitely going to take too long and Dennis
refused. I was back to square one so I got down on my knees
and begged again. I gave him the money and hoped for the
best. I was elated when he returned with the big white box in
his grease covered hands. I took the box and ran right
downstairs and put it in the freezer.

Four days later, on July 30th, I called Tim to wish him a
happy birthday. He really sounded down in the dumps. In a
sullen voice he said, "Thanks." I inquired if anything was
wrong. He replied in an even more sullen voice, "No." I was

feeling bad enough that I wasn't there for his birthday but this was really getting to me. I said, "Did you find your birthday surprise in the freezer?" I heard a despondent, "Yes." I said, "Tim, what is wrong?" He said, "My birthday cake says 'Happy Birthday Asshole'!" I was mortified. I couldn't believe his brother could have done such a thing and to think he thought I did it. I still cannot believe that Dennis had the nerve to ask those lovely young girls that work in the ice cream store to write that on the cake. It didn't even phase Dennis. He thought it was hysterical. To make matters worse, friends invited Tim over for dinner on his birthday and he took the cake with him for dessert.

Growing up the boys were allowed to select their favorite birthday cake. Some liked yellow cake with chocolate icing and some liked devil's food with butter cream icing. Every year Tim picked angel food cake which I hated to make. It wasn't until he was in his twenties that he confided to me that he really never liked angel food cake. In response to why he always chose it I was informed that because all of his brothers detested angel food cake he got to eat the whole thing.

31. MIDNIGHT VISITOR

When Jeff, Kevin & Keith moved to Texas, Tim and Dennis took over the large bedroom downstairs. They were home from college for the summer. Our Father was awakened in the middle of the night. He heard noises in the kitchen but there were no lights on. He ventured down the hallway and cautiously peered into the kitchen. The refrigerator door was open and the light reflected a person with long dark hair bent over looking for food. As Our Father recounted to me later, "The whole ass end of his pants were split open!"

This happened shortly after the Manson murders so it really gave Our Father a scare. He watched the figure for a few moments before shouting, "What are you doing?" The person jumped two feet and spun around. Our Father was relieved to see it was a girl but she was disheveled and had scratches and blood on herself and her tattered clothing. He asked, "Who are you?" She replied, "Your son said I could spend the night here." He asked, "Which son?" She said, "I don't know his name." Our Father said, "We'll see about this. Come with me."

They paraded down the stairs to the bedroom where he turned on the light. Tim and Dennis were both asleep and the sofa in the bedroom had been turned into a makeshift bed. Dennis jumped out of bed and said, "I can explain everything. She crashed her motorcycle on 1-95 and was lying on the side of the road. I stopped to help her and suggested she come here for the night and I would take her back in the daylight and help her get her motorcycle running again."

I realized what Dennis did was very kind and caring but I was a nervous wreck over the whole thing. I had to leave for work before Dennis and his waif left for the motorcycle. I just knew when Dennis took her back to 1-95 that a whole army of Hell's Angels were going to be waiting there to find out who took their "Old Lady" home for the night.

67

32.   SNAKE EYES

Unfortunately, Our Father had a heart attack in 1983. Although we were elated to learn that he had a heart, it was a very grim time for us all. While Our Father was recuperating, friends brought him a beautiful basket of fruit. It had everything in it from a cantaloupe to a bunch of bananas.

After the friends departed, Dennis asked if he could sample the fruit. He made a hole in the cellophane wrapping on the basket which was sitting on the floor. We were watching TV. I was sitting on the sofa and thought I saw something move on the floor next to me. I glanced down, screamed and jumped up on top of the coffee table. I kept pointing and screaming, "Five snakes." Kevin said, "She's wrong. There's seven snakes."

Our Father clutched his heart as Dennis ran over to pick them up. As soon as he touched one, the rest headed in different directions. Dennis flushed the first one down the toilet and joined in the search for the other six. They had obviously crawled out of the fruit basket. I remained on top of the coffee table in a state of apoplexy until they were all found and placed in a large jar with holes punched in the top and deposited outdoors.

Naturally after that ordeal I had to go to the bathroom. As I went to sit on the toilet the first snake found was coiling up out of the toilet bowl. I haven't used a bathroom since that day without checking out the toilet bowl first.

Snakes remind me of a trip to the Zoo with our sons during Christmas vacation, 1968. It was the first time I had been in the city since the riots and I was a little apprehensive. The only thing the boys talked about was seeing the monkeys. The first place we visited was the snake house. After seeing a few snakes the boys started whining, "Where are the monkeys?" "We want to see some monkeys." We continued through the snake house until one of them yelled, "I see the monkeys," and they all started running. It was an empty snake cage and a man was sitting inside with his legs curled up washing the inside of the glass. We were so embarrassed. We gathered them together and flew to the monkey house.

33. SPANKY

When Kevin moved back home he bought a Pit Bull against our wishes. His name was Spanky. He had one blue eye and one brown eye. Despite the reputation of Pit Bulls, Spanky wasn't vicious. He only had one major problem. He attacked tires on moving vehicles.

A friend that sold Avon products had her husband drop off my order on his way to work. When he backed down our driveway Spanky was running around his car. About a mile from our house he had his first flat tire. By the time he arrived late for work he had repaired all four tires. No one at work believed his story. On his way home he stopped at our house to inquire if our dog had ever bitten anyone's tires. Naturally I let Kevin answer that question. The man was so relieved. He said his co-workers said he was crazy. No dog could bite all four tires. A week later Kevin received the bill for the four tires. In all, he replaced twenty-three tires during Spanky's brief stay at our house.

We never could figure out how he could attack tires on moving vehicles without spinning around himself or at the very least losing his teeth. The worst event was The Case of the Trans Am. Those two tires cost $180.00. Some people took it in stride and asked to be compensated. The Trans Am driver, however, threatened our lives.

34. MISSING PLANES

Our boys had real problems with flying. Dennis spent a
summer in Texas working with his brothers. He notified us he
would be arriving home at 11:00 a.m. at BWI airport. We
went to 8:00 Mass and drove directly to the airport.

The plane arrived on time and we watched hundreds of
travelers disembark. Everyone except Dennis. When the last
person came through the gate I said, "Excuse me. Is there
anyone else on the plane?" The lady assured me she was the
last person. She added, "Oh, before we left Dallas someone
got on the plane and announced that if someone was willing to
give up their seat they would receive a free ticket plus they
would be able to fly out on the next flight." Our Father and I
shook our heads. Of course Dennis had given up his seat for a
free ticket to anywhere.

We went to the airline desk and inquired as to the name of
the passenger that had given up his seat. Well, it wasn't
Dennis. The clerk informed us that Dennis was on the
passenger list. Since it was a non-stop flight there was only
one explanation and only I could think of it. He had fallen out
of the plane somewhere between Dallas and Baltimore. The
clerk was concerned. She called Dallas airport and they
confirmed that he was on the plane. She finally suggested that
we call our sons in Dallas and she handed me the phone. I
dialed the number and Dennis answered. He had missed the
plane. He had called us but we had already left for Church.
Now he would be arriving at 8:00 p.m.

He did arrive at 8:00 but his baggage did not. Everything
he owned was in Our Father's U. S. Army duffel bag which
failed to show up. We spent an hour filling out baggage claim
reports. Someone from the airline took Dennis to the back
room where the baggage originates and sure enough there was

71

his bag wedged between the opening and the wall.

On the way home from the airport Dennis related what else happened that day. He was sitting in the Dallas airport waiting to depart. He laid his magazine and plane ticket on his seat and went to the Men's Room. When he returned his ticket was gone. He rushed to the ticket agent and explained his plight. The agent was quite sympathetic but informed him he would have to purchase another ticket. The airline did refund his money thirty days later.

Our Father and Tim went to Dulles airport to pick up Jeff. Jeff called shortly after they left to tell me he made a terrible mistake. He was arriving at BWI and departing from Dulles. I had to call Dulles and have Our Father paged so I could tell him he had to leave Dulles and drive two hours to BWI to pick up his son.

Jeff and Keith both flew home for Thanksgiving. They both lived in the same house and both were flying home for Thanksgiving. One was arriving at 1:00 p.m. at Dulles Airport (about an hour and a half away from our home in Maryland) and the other was arriving at 1:15 p.m. at BWI (about forty minutes away in the opposite direction). Maybe you can figure that one out!

35. ERIN GO BRAHLESS

A dear friend of ours died of cancer in 1976. He left a wife and four teenage sons. We got together frequently because between us we had nine teenage sons. A year later Joan called me to tell me she was going to Ireland with a group of relatives. She was apprehensive because she would have to stay in a hotel room alone. Our Father suggested that I go along on the trip and share the room with Joan. I was elated. I always wanted to visit Ireland and this would probably be my only chance.

We landed at Shannon Airport. I couldn't wait to get to Ireland to hear the Irish music. We walked through the airport to the strains of Stevie Wonder singing "You Are the Sunshine of my Life." We were assigned four to a rental car and since our other two passengers didn't drive it meant Joan or I would have to. I totally refused to drive on the wrong side of the road so that left Joan. She pulled the lever for the emergency break and the hood went up. I got out and closed it. Again she pulled the lever and again I got out. This went on for so long that we were assigned to another car and never drove again.

We spent fifteen days traveling around the countryside. The following is an excerpt from my Trip Diary, April 17, 1977:

"After church we went to Blarney. After climbing to the top of the castle, we kissed the Blarney Stone and made a wish. Apparently I made the wrong wish because two minutes later I fell on my ass and may never be the same."

Rosses Point in County Sligo was my favorite spot in Ireland. The hotel was situated with Sligo Bay on two sides. From the sliding glass door you could see lighthouses, whitecaps, green grass, mountains and islands. It was an unbelievable sight.

Speaking of unbelievable sights, after showering I opened the bathroom door. Joan was standing in the dressing area putting on makeup. Being very modest I held the towel in front of me and backed across the room so Joan couldn't see anything. I glanced around for my suitcase and, much to my horror, saw a tour bus loaded with tourists parked in front of our window. I had mooned the whole bus. But the important thing is Joan didn't see a thing!

36. URGE TO DIRGE

My brother, Jack, only owns one suit. I would calculate it to be approximately fifty-two years old. It is so out of style it makes the Nehru jacket avant garde. He only wears it to weddings and funerals because he spends his winters on Florida beaches and his summers on the beach in Wildwood.

When my dear Aunt Marie died the funeral was in northwest Washington, D.C. and the cemetery was forty-five minutes away in northeast D. C. Naturally my brother attended the funeral in "the suit." The funeral procession exited the church parking lot and proceeded across town until the car in front of us ran out of gas. Only a son of mine would be in a funeral procession with an empty tank. We had to wait for Dennis and his brothers to push the car off the street and crowd into other cars so the procession could continue.

When the ceremony was over we all walked toward our cars (everyone except Dennis, of course). My brother approached Dennis and said, "Hey, Dennis, I've got a gas can in the trunk of my car." Dennis replied, "Uncle Jack, I've got a suit in mine!"

Our Father often recalls his most memorable experience as an Altar Boy. He loved to serve at funerals because they were always on weekdays and he could be excused from school for an hour. One of the parishioners, who had been wheelchair-bound most of her life, passed away. The coffin was placed in front of the altar. The Altar Boys assisted the priest as he sprinkled holy water over the bier. Suddenly the casket flew open and the woman sat straight up. While the bereaved were screaming and passing out, the funeral director rushed up the center aisle and proceeded to stuff her body back into the casket and forced it closed. It's quite fortunate that Our Father lived across the street from the church because he immediately ran home and changed his pants.

37. TWO SEATS IN THE BALCONY

Our Father and I spent a few days in New Bern, North Carolina. Our accommodations included a room with a balcony overlooking the harbor. Our villa was on the second floor so we had a beautiful view of the boats and water.

It was a very mild evening so we fixed a drink and sat on our balcony. The balconies were separated by concrete walls between each villa. Around 11:00 P.M. we decided to retire to our room. Unfortunately we were locked out. Although we were on the second floor, the villas were built on pilings so our balcony was sixteen feet from the ground. Jumping was out.

I knew Our Father could get us out of this mess because he always did. Our only recourse was to get onto the balcony next-door. Since I was smaller Our Father suggested that I be the one to make the trip. It meant climbing over the railing and hoisting my body around the concrete wall. I had to straddle the wall with my left leg over my railing and my right leg over the neighbor's railing. Our Father assured me he wouldn't let go of me. It was a hair raising experience but I made it safely.

The worse was yet to come. I now had to knock on the door. Picture yourself laying in bed watching TV sixteen feet off the ground and someone knocks on your balcony door. A female voice weakly asked, "Who is it?" I answered, "I live next-door but I'm locked out. Could you please call Security?" The lady reluctantly opened the door but not before asking, "How in the world did you ever get onto my balcony?" I let her know it wasn't easy. I went through her unit and waited at my front door until Security arrived and freed Our Father from bondage.

38. HURRICANE KLAUS

Our Father and I decided to spend our 30th wedding anniversary on the island of St. Maarten. Since we were married in St. Martin's Church on November 11th (St. Martin's Day) it seemed appropriate. We invited friends who were also celebrating thirty years of marriage to join us.

We arrived at our villa and Our Father was the first to use the bathroom. He rushed into the living room and announced, "The next time I use the bathroom you're coming with me and holding on to me." It had a suction toilet. All of us had to go into the bathroom for a demonstration. Our Father flushed the toilet and it actually pulled the bathroom door open. It made for an interesting week.

We signed up for a sailing trip to St. Bart's for Wednesday but it rained all night and Wednesday morning it became torrential. The sailing trip was canceled so we decided to go shopping. I was amazed at how many stores were closed on a week day. I was in a store and they announced they were closing in fifteen minutes. I approached a salesperson to find out why. She said, "The big wave is coming." I was baffled. The next store had a radio on and it was then that I learned Hurricane Klaus was approaching the island.

We hurried to our car and headed for the grocery store. The shelves were practically bare but we managed to pick up some staples to hold us over. At the villa the maid brought us extra towels and candles. The pool was right outside our door and we refused to be cooped up inside on our vacation so we jumped into the pool. It wasn't long before our villa neighbors joined us one by one. The only thing getting pelted with rain was our heads. It was great fun and we got to meet a lot of people we normally wouldn't have. When our skin began to shrivel up we returned to the villa but not for long.

Our next stop was a nearby bar on the beach. We figured

as long as they had power we could eat, drink and be merry. The Caribbean was really churning up by now. The boats were rocking endlessly. The crew from one of the boats were in the bar. A father and son had decided to ride out the storm anchored out but they brought the crew ashore.

It was such an exciting atmosphere. As the waves rolled closer and closer we would get up, pick up the table and chairs, and move further back. All good times must come to an end but not until we looked outside and saw the water was up to the doors of our rental car. We were forced to return to the villa. There was no power and you couldn't flush the toilet.

The bedroom ceiling leaked profusely. We kept moving the bed around the room to keep it dry. All you have to do is tell me I can't use the bathroom and all hell breaks loose. I woke up in the middle of the night with cramps. What the hell was I going to do? Our Father found a solution. He put a plastic bag in the trash can and sat me out on the balcony in the middle of a hurricane.

The following day we drove into town. The sights were incredible. There were hundreds of boats helter skelter along the beach. The sailboat we were supposed to go to St. Bart's on was upside down on the sand. There was at least two feet of seaweed all over the boats and beach. What a sight!

It rained six out of seven days we were there. We came home without a suntan but with a volume of memories.

39. MALE STRIPPER

When I retired from the school system four teachers were retiring at the same time. The faculty gave us a lovely retirement dinner. The students gave us a retirement party. Several days later the faculty was summoned to the gallery after the students had been dismissed.

There was a man in front of the room in a three piece suit with a clipboard in his hand. I assumed he was from the Board of Education and was going to make some sort of presentation. The five retirees were invited to sit in the front. The man in the three piece suit turned on music and proceeded to take off his clothes. Someone had hired a male stripper. I was mortified. I turned to the teacher next to me whose husband is a Rabbi and said, "When I find out who did this I'm going to strangle them." When he finished gyrating around the room he said, "Now I guess you ladies would like to know who gave you this wonderful gift?" I blurted out, "We certainly would." He smiled and said, "Tim and Dennis McLaughlin!"

40.   SOLD TO THE HIGHEST BIDDER

We had an auction and sold all of our furniture, antiques, junk, etc. in anticipation of moving to our new home in Virginia. Before the auction we told all of our sons if there was anything they wanted to speak up before the auction. They didn't want anything.

I had a deacon's bench that I used for a coffee table in the family room.   The boys were not allowed to put their feet on it and they couldn't place a glass on it without a coaster.

The auction was held in our backyard. We had a deck across the back of the house on the second level where Our Father our close friends and I viewed the event. I heard, "Hey Mom, look what I bought." I looked down on the patio and saw Kevin with my deacon's bench. He was standing on it, walking on it, jumping on it and dancing on it. I nearly fell off the deck. I guess he had been waiting for years to do that.

41. HEAD WEDGE

While building our retirement home we lived in a small house in the same community. Our Father kept his classic Chris Craft in the garage of the new house for winter storage. While I was playing golf he decided to move the boat over to where we were living so he could get it all spiffy for the season. He backed a flatbed truck up to the boat. He then attempted to hook the boat trailer to the truck hitch. In doing so the boat came over the chocks and pinned his head between the trailer and the truck. He was bent over, bleeding from somewhere, and totally helpless. There was nobody within yelling distance and I was twenty miles away.

Dizziness was setting in and with it the realization that he was going to die if something wasn't done soon. He doesn't know how he did it but he says he mustered up a "super strength" and pushed the trailer and boat enough to get his head out of the vise. He had cuts and scratches on both sides of his temple.

That evening he suggested that we take a little cruise down to the Bay in our other boat Cirrhosis of the River. On our trip back home the boat started spiting and sputtering. I prayed we would make it to our pier. We almost did. The boat died before we could tie up and the current carried us down stream. Our Father always knew what to do in such situations but I was traumatized when he jumped overboard leaving me alone on the boat. He told me to throw him a rope. He then swam back to our pier towing the boat with a rope. He tied up the boat and I climbed ashore.

He was standing in the boat holding a wet sock in each hand when he asked, "Where am I?". I figured he had sustained a concussion from his adventure earlier in the day which caused Amnesia. I tried to coax him out of the boat but he refused to leave until he found out where he was. It took at least thirty minutes to convince him to leave the boat.

After two days in the hospital, EKG, MRI and several other tests it was concluded that he had suffered from Hypothermia. After the diagnosis one of our sons called to say they were having a new event in the Olympics and that he should try out for it. He said it was a type of biathlon. You had to bend over, keep your head wedged in a vise for an hour and then jump in the water and tow a boat for a mile while swimming ashore. If there had been such an event I know Our Father would have won hands down.

42. SOUTHERN ICE

February is one month of the year that I could do without.
I remember a February that the sun did not shine once
throughout the entire month. When we moved to our
waterfront retirement home I wondered how I would endure
that month. No swimming, boating, golfing on the agenda.
Our Father alleviated my fears by promising we would spend
February in Florida every year.

The night before we were to leave on our first February
evacuation the weather man forecast a snowstorm. We woke
up to blizzard conditions. I wanted to postpone the trip but
Our Father thought it was the perfect travel day. Schools and
offices would be closed and little traffic on the roads.
Naturally I believed him.

The roads were so bad you couldn't drive over twenty miles
per hour. I was assured that things would improve when we
got to the Interstate. Ha! I 95 had only one lane cleared all
the way through the state of North Carolina. South Carolina,
however, was a horse of a different color. South Carolina
didn't have snow. It had ice--a foot of ice. They also had no
equipment to clear the roads.

Darkness had fallen and so had four eighteen wheelers
upside down along the highway. Our Father decided it was
time to exit I 95 and find a motel. We joined the procession of
cars sliding down the ramp to find a motel that sensible people
had filled hours before. That night I learned first hand the
meaning of the words, "There is no room in the Inn." After
being turned away from six motels we returned to the Interstate which was the second major mistake of the day.

Traffic was virtually at a standstill. If you touched the

accelerator you slid either left or right--not straight. Nothing was open because no one could drive to work to open the restaurants, rest stops, gas stations, etc. An RV on I 95 was allowing car passengers to come aboard and use the bathroom. I prayed excessively and Our Father put his seat belt on for the first time since they were invented. It took an hour and a half to get to the next exit. This time we were exiting permanently even if we had to sleep in the car. We kept driving at a snail's pace on a secondary road until we happened upon a State Trooper with his light twirling. He gave us directions to the local high school in Tuborville that had opened up a shelter for stranded drivers. What a welcome sight that was.

The Red Cross provided blankets and people slept on the floor and bleachers in the auditorium. We were one of the lucky ones. We were issued a wrestling mat to sleep on. The Red Cross also provided coffee and donuts. The Town Council and volunteers worked all night to provide everyone with the finest Southern hospitality you could ask for.

While standing in the lobby smoking I overheard one of the volunteers tell his wife he was taking her to dinner the next day to a place she hadn't been to in years. When she asked, "Where?", he replied, "Your kitchen." That made my day.

43. BRICKLAYER'S FOUNDATION

Jeff is a masonry subcontractor and lives in Maryland. Instead of buying him a birthday present and mailing it to Maryland, I decided to order something from a popular catalog and have it sent directly to him. I finally decided on two pairs of summer shorts. I had them forwarded to him with a gift card enclosed, "Love, Mom and Dad."

I happened to be in Maryland visiting my grandchildren the following week. Jeff stopped by. He had the birthday package with him. He said, "Thanks for my present but what am I supposed to do with it?" He handed me the package. I opened it and found a satin one-piece bra/girdle foundation and a card that said, "Love, Mom and Dad." He added, "How am I supposed to explain this to my roommates who were home when I opened it?" I absolutely could not believe my eyes. He felt better when I told him I ordered him two pairs of shorts but that the store made a terrible mistake. He had already discussed Mom's apparent senility with his brothers. Believe me, I read the Riot Act to the catalog company. Be very careful when you send a gift directly to the giftee.

44. FINIS!

I would like to leave you with a few more stories that don't warrant a chapter but, nonetheless, are worth mentioning.

A small child came into my office on her way to class. She was holding a box and wanted to show me what she had brought for Show and Tell. I peeked into the box and saw an ugly little frog. I said, "What's its name, Nancy?" She said, "Mrs. McLaughlin." I was overwhelmed with flattery and asked why she had named it that. She answered, "Because it looks like you."

Keith had an after school job at a Shell station in Ashton. Tim worked for an Esso station in Wheaton. For extra money Keith would sometimes help out at the Esso station. To protect his clothing he would wear his Shell uniform. It had his name and the Shell logo on the pocket. One day a disgruntled customer told the owner of the Esso station that service was so poor at his station that last week a kid from the Shell station across the street had to come over and put gas in his car.

Jeff has always been a neatnik. His house is immaculate. He washes his truck before he goes to work. He vacuums his boat before he takes it out. I was explaining to my two pregnant daughters-in-law that my first baby was two weeks late. Tim popped up with, "If I know Jeff, he was too busy cleaning his womb."

I am very happy to report that I survived raising five teenage sons. There were times when I didn't think I would make it. To this day, if the phone rings during the night I sit straight up in the bed. I never had a tranquilizer and I didn't even get an ulcer out of the deal. My friend, Gail, after describing her latest crisis would say to me, "I nearly had a rag baby." I was never really sure what that meant. If it means what I think it means I must have at least a thousand rag babies out there floating around somewhere.

Now I am embarking on my final chapter in life which includes my seven beautiful grandchildren. Our Father always admonished our sons with, "I hope when you grow up you have five sons so you'll know what we're going through." Dennis has almost fulfilled Our Father's dream. He now has four sons. Of course our grandchildren are being raised entirely different. No such thing as a spanking--only Time Out. Everything that Mi Mi and Pop Pop say is politically incorrect.

There is an Irish Blessing on my refrigerator door

Grandchildren are gifts of God.

It is God's Way...

Of compensating us for growing old.

My cousin, Patty, has an even better observation. She professes, "Grandchildren are God's reward for not killing your own."